# Dinosaurs

The Nature Company Discoveries Library published by Time-Life Books

Conceived and produced by
Weldon Owen Pty Limited
43 Victoria Street, McMahons Point,
NSW, 2060, Australia
A member of the
Weldon Owen Group of Companies
Sydney • San Francisco
Copyright © 1995 US Weldon Owen Inc.
Copyright © 1995 Weldon Owen Pty Limited
Reprinted 1996 (three times), 1997

THE NATURE COMPANY
Priscilla Wrubel, Ed Strobin, Steve Manning,
Georganne Papac, Tracy Fortini

TIME-LIFE BOOKS
Time-Life Books is a division of Time Life Inc.
Time-Life is a trademark of Time Warner Inc.
U.S.A.

Time-Life Custom Publishing
**Vice President and Publisher:** Terry Newell
**Director of New Product Development:**
Quentin McAndrew
**Managing Editor:** Donia Ann Steele
**Director of Sales:** Neil Levin
**Director of Financial Operations:** J. Brian Birky

WELDON OWEN Pty Limited
**Chairman:** Kevin Weldon
**President:** John Owen
**Publisher:** Sheena Coupe
**Managing Editor:** Rosemary McDonald
**Project Editor:** Kathy Gerrard
**Text Editor:** Claire Craig
**Educational Consultants:** Richard L. Needham,
Deborah A. Powell
**Art Director:** Sue Burk
**Designer:** Kathy Gammon
**Assistant Designer:** Melissa Wilton
**Visual Research Coordinator:** Jenny Mills

**Picture Research:** Annette Crueger
**Illustrations Research:** Peter Barker
**Production Manager:** Caroline Webber
**Production Assistant** Kylie Lawson
**Vice President, International Sales:**
Stuart Laurence
**Coeditions Director:** Derek Barton

**Text:** Carson Creagh

**Illustrators:** Simone End, Christer Eriksson,
John Francis, David Kirshner, Frank Knight,
James McKinnon, Colin Newman, Paul Newman,
Wendy de Paauw, Marilyn Pride, Andrew
Robinson/Garden Studio, Peter Schouten,
Ray Sim, Rod Westblade

Library of Congress
Cataloging-in-Publication Data
Dinosaurs / consulting editor, Angela Milner.

        p. cm -- (Discoveries Library)

    Includes index.
    ISBN 0-7835-4765-X
    1. Dinosaurs--Juvenile literature. [1.
    Dinosaurs.] I. Milner, Angela C. II. Series:
    Discoveries Library (Alexandria, VA.)

    QE862.D5D516  1995
    567.9' 1--dc20              95-12938

Manufactured by Mandarin Offset
Printed in China

A Weldon Owen Production

THE NATURE COMPANY
DISCOVERIES
L I B R A R Y

# Dinosaurs

CONSULTING EDITOR

## Dr. Angela Milner

Head of the Fossil Vertebrates and Anthropology Division
Natural History Museum, London, England

TIME
LIFE
BOOKS

# Contents

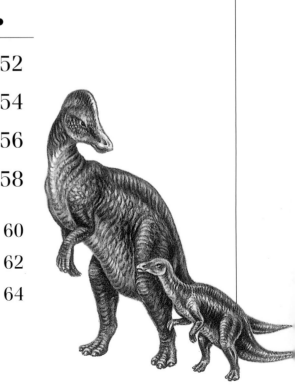

**Blue-green algae and bacteria**

**Soft-bodied organisms**
Fossils of algae, bacteria and jellyfish are rare. Their soft bodies usually rotted quickly, before mud could harden on them.

**Animals with shells**
Between 570 and 250 million years ago, there were more than 10,000 kinds of trilobites. They ranged from 1 in (3 cm) to 1½ ft (50 cm) in length.

Jellyfish

Ammonite

Trilobites

Pteraspis

Drepanaspis

# Before the Dinosaurs

Life on Earth began 4,600 million years ago. Its long history is divided into different periods, during which an amazing variety of life forms developed or died out. In the beginning, single-celled algae and bacteria formed, or evolved, in the warm seas that covered most of the planet.

In the Paleozoic Era, more complex plants and animals appeared in the sea: worms, jellyfish and hard-shelled mollusks swarmed in shallow waters and were eaten by bony fish. When plants and animals first appeared on land, they were eaten by amphibians that had evolved from fish with lungs and strong fins. Some amphibians then evolved into reptiles that did not lay their eggs in water. Early reptiles developed into turtles and tortoises, lizards, crocodiles, birds and the first dinosaurs. They dominated the world for millions of years.

**The first jawless fish**
Armor-plated fish such as *Pteraspis* and *Drepanaspis* did not have jaws. They sucked up food from the mud or fed on plankton.

**A bony fish**
*Dunkleosteus*, a giant of late Devonian seas, grew to 11 feet (3.4 m). It grasped its prey in sharp, bony dental plates because it did not have teeth.

Scorpion

**An amphibian**
*Ichthyostega* could not expand or contract its solid rib cage. This 3-ft (1-m) long amphibian had to use its mouth to push air into its lungs.

**An early reptile**
*Hylonomus*, a 3-in (20-cm) long reptile, is known only from fossils found in the remains of hollow tree trunks, where it may have become trapped while hunting insects.

**A mammal-like reptile**
*Dimetrodon*, which was 10 ft (3 m) long, may have angled its "sail" to catch sunlight so that it could warm up quickly in the morning.

**Thecodontian archosaurs**
*Ornithosuchus* looked like *Tyrannosaurus*, but it was not a dinosaur. It had five toes on each hind foot while *Tyrannosaurus* had only three.

## THE DINOSAUR RACE

Dinosaurs, which appeared in the Triassic Period, were descended from crocodile-like reptiles, whose legs sprawled at right angles from their bodies. *Euparkeria*, from the early Triassic Period, had straighter legs and carried its body off the ground. The legs of *Lagosuchus*, from the middle Triassic Period, were tucked beneath its body, and it walked on its hind legs. By the late Triassic Period, the predator *Ornithosuchus* looked a little like a dinosaur, but the earliest known dinosaur was *Eoraptor*. It appeared 228 million years ago.

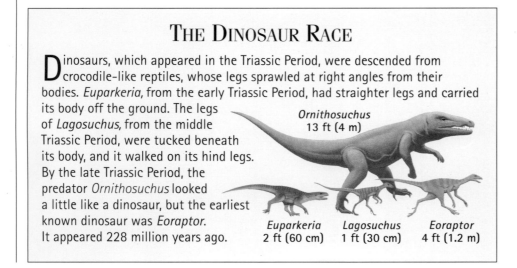

Ornithosuchus
13 ft (4 m)

Euparkeria
2 ft (60 cm)

Lagosuchus
1 ft (30 cm)

Eoraptor
4 ft (1.2 m)

| millions of years ago | 4,600 | 2,500 | 570 | 510 | 439 | 408 | 362 | 290 | 245 |
|---|---|---|---|---|---|---|---|---|---|
| | Precambrian Era | | Paleozoic Era | | | | | | |
| Origin of the Earth | Archaean | Proterozoic | Cambrian | Ordovician | Silurian | Devonian | Carboniferous | Permian |
| |  | | | | | | | |
| | First algae and single-celled bacteria appeared in the seas. | First animals with soft bodies and many cells. They looked like worms and jellyfish. | First sponges, segmented worms and hard-shelled animals. | First animals with backbones; jawless fish, then sharks and bony fish. | First land plants. Sea scorpions up to 7 ft (2 m) dominated the seas. | The Age of Fishes and the first land animals with backbones. | The Age of Amphibians. Primitive reptiles hunted insects and small amphibians. | Many species of reptiles that ate plants and meat. Trilobites disappear. |

Dunkleosteus

Ichthyostega

Dimetrodon

Dragonfly

Hylonomus

Ornithosuchus

# What is a Dinosaur?

**D**inosaurs were very special reptiles. Some were the size of chickens; others may have been as long as jumbo jets. These creatures were the most successful animals that have ever lived on Earth. They dominated the world for nearly 150 million years and were found on every continent during the Mesozoic Era, which is divided into the Triassic, Jurassic and Cretaceous periods. Like reptiles today, dinosaurs had scaly skin and their eggs had shells. The earliest dinosaurs ate meat, while later plant-eating dinosaurs enjoyed the lush plant life around them. Dinosaurs are called "lizard-hipped" or "bird-hipped," depending on how their hip bones were arranged. They stood on either four legs or two and walked with straight legs tucked beneath their bodies. Dinosaurs are the only reptiles that have ever been able to do this.

**JURASSIC HUNTERS**
In a scene from the Jurassic Period in North America, 69-ft (21-m) long *Apatosaurus* munches on a cycad as a 7-ft (2-m) long *Ornitholestes* pounces on a salamander disturbed by the grazing giant.

## DID YOU KNOW?

The term "dinosaur," which means "terrible lizard," was invented in 1841 by Sir Richard Owen, a famous British scientist. He was the first person to realize that these fascinating reptiles were different from living reptiles and should be placed in a separate group.

A Dinosaur Family Tree

CRETACEOUS
JURASSIC
TRIASSIC
LATE PERMIAN

Ceratosaurs: *Coelophysis*
Carnosaurs: *Tyrannosaurus*
Coelurosaurs: *Coelurus, Ornithomimus, Dromaeosaurus*
Birds
Prosauropods: *Plateosaurus*
Sauropods: *Diplodocus, Brachiosaurus*
Stegosaurs: *Stegosaurus*
Ankylosaurs: *Ankylosaurus, Euoplocephalus*
Ornithopods: *Pachycephalosaurus, Iguanodon, Parasaurolophus*
Ceratopians: *Protoceratops, Triceratops*

145
208
245

Theropods (meat eaters)     Sauropodomorphs (plant eaters)     Armored plant eaters     Other plant eaters

Saurischians (lizard-hipped dinosaurs)          Ornithischians (bird-hipped dinosaurs)

Archosaurs (ancestors to dinosaurs, pterosaurs, crocodiles)

**DINOSAUR FAMILIES**
This family tree shows how paleontologists divide dinosaurs into different groups.

# DINOSAUR LOOKALIKES

*Scaphognathus*

Look carefully at these animals. Do you think they are dinosaurs? They are certainly prehistoric and they may resemble dinosaurs physically, but in fact none of them is a dinosaur. Pterosaurs such as *Scaphognathus*, which had a wingspan of about 3 ft (1 m), lived in the late Triassic Period. *Dimetrodon*, a mammal-like reptile, died out before dinosaurs evolved. *Kronosaurus*, a marine predator of the early Cretaceous Period, was twice as long as a great white shark.

*Dimetrodon*

*Kronosaurus*

Pleistocene 1.64–0.01
Pliocene 5–1.64
Holocene 0.01–now
Miocene 23–5
Oligocene 35–23
Eocene 56–35
Paleocene 65–56

CENOZOIC

Cretaceous 145–65
Jurassic 208–145
Triassic 245–208

MESOZOIC

Permian 290–245
Carboniferous 362–290
Devonian 408–362

LATE PALEOZOIC

Silurian 439–408
Ordovician 510–439
Cambrian 570–510

EARLY PALEOZOIC

millions of years ago

**SLICES OF LIFE**
Dinosaurs lived on Earth for about 150 million years—almost 40 times longer than the human race that studies them.

*Discover more in* Fossilized Clues

# Dinosaur Hips

## SPRAWLING

The ancestors of the dinosaurs sprawled on four legs, like a lizard. They had to use large amounts of energy to twist the whole body and lift each leg in turn.

## HALFWAY UP

Some reptiles, such as today's crocodiles, have upright hind legs. As their bodies are off the ground, they can run on their hind legs for short distances.

## ON TWO LEGS

A dinosaur's weight was supported easily by its straight legs, tucked under its body. As the body weight was balanced over the hips by the weight of the tail, some dinosaurs were bipedal (two-legged) and used their hands for grasping.

## TWO-LEGGED PLANT EATER

This 43-ft (13-m) long *Edmontosaurus* has a typical ornithischian pelvis. The pubis points backwards and allows more space for the large intestines that plant eaters needed to digest their food. Conversely, in sauropods (plant-eating saurischians) the intestines are slung forward. This means the forward-pointing pubis does not get in the way of these four-legged (quadrupedal) dinosaurs.

Dinosaurs walked upright with their legs beneath their bodies. No other reptiles have been able to do this. Dinosaurs had a right-angled joint at the top of the leg bone that fit into a hole in the hip bones. This allowed the limbs to be positioned under the body, so the weight of the dinosaur was supported, and all the joints worked as simple forward and backward hinges. These evolutionary advances were the key to the great success of the dinosaurs. They did not have to throw the whole body from side to side to move their legs, so they could breathe easily while running quickly. They were able to grow bigger, walk further and move faster than any other reptiles. The two main groups of dinosaurs had different kinds of hips. The meat eaters and plant-eating sauropods (called saurischians, or lizard-hipped dinosaurs) had a forward-pointing pubis. In the plant-eating ornithischians, or bird-hipped dinosaurs, part of the pubis pointed backward, to allow more space for the gut.

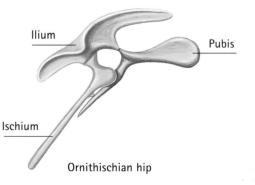

Ilium

Pubis

Ischium

Ornithischian hip

Alligator

## EVOLVING SIDE BY SIDE

Some dinosaurs were called "bird-hipped", but this does not mean that birds have the same kinds of hips as these dinosaurs, even though their hips look similar. A bird walks on its hind legs, with its body tipped forward and supported in the same way as two-legged dinosaurs. Birds, however, actually evolved from lizard-hipped dinosaurs. An alligator's hip bones look similar to those of a lizard-hipped dinosaur because they had common ancestors.

Starling

## STRANGE BUT TRUE

Fossils sometimes reveal illnesses, accidents and injuries. Sometime in the early Cretaceous Period, an *Iguanodon* fractured its hip. The dinosaur recovered, but was left with a bulge of new bone around the fracture.

Healed fracture

## FAST-MOVING HUNTER

This fierce, 39-ft (12-m) long, meat-eating *Allosaurus* from the late Jurassic Period was a saurischian. Its pubis pointed forward between the legs and with the other pelvic bones (ilium and ischium) formed a rigid triangle to support the leg muscles for fast running.

**Ilium**
Supported the leg muscles. It transferred leg movement to the rest of the body.

**Pubis**
Pointed forward. It helped to support the strong leg muscles in both meat and plant eaters.

**Ischium**
Pointed backward. It supported muscles that carried the tail off the ground.

Femur

Tibia

Saurischian hip

11

**Longest-winged pterosaur**
*Pteranodon* had a long, toothless beak. It probably scooped up fish in its narrow jaws, just like a pelican.

**Fish eater**
*Dimorphodon*, a pterosaur, had a long tail and forward-facing teeth to grasp its prey.

**Pint-sized flier**
*Archaeopteryx,* the earliest bird of all, evolved from the dinosaurs. It probably ate insects and small reptiles.

**TARGET IN SIGHT**
Above the seas in the late Jurassic Period, one of the most common pterosaurs, *Rhamphorhynchus*, spies *Muraenosaurus*, a 20-ft (6-m) long plesiosaur, attacking a school of *Leptolepis* fish. *Rhamphorhynchus* had a leaf-shaped membrane on the end of its tail to help it steer in flight.

# In the Sea and in the Air

During the Mesozoic Era, dinosaurs ruled the land, marine reptiles dominated the sea and flying reptiles, called pterosaurs, glided through the skies. Marine reptiles and pterosaurs were only distant cousins of the dinosaurs, even though some marine reptiles looked almost like long-necked sauropods with fins. Pterosaurs were the first animals with backbones to take to the air—on wings made of skin. Many of them hunted fish, but others such as *Quetzalcoatlus,* the largest flying animal of all time, had no teeth and used their jaws to eat decaying animals. Plesiosaurs, pliosaurs, marine turtles, crocodiles and other sea reptiles lived in the waters of the Mesozoic world. The plesiosaurs had long necks and ate small sea creatures, while the big-headed, short-necked pliosaurs tackled larger prey with their strong teeth and jaws.

## WORLDS APART

There were differences among the flying animals of the Mesozoic Era—differences that can still be seen in flying creatures today. The wings of a pterosaur were skin membranes, supported by a long fourth finger. The wings of a living bat are also made of skin membrane. However, a bat's wings are supported by all its fingers. Modern birds evolved from *Archaeopteryx*. Its wings were made of feathers that were arranged in a similar way to those of a living bird, such as a pigeon.

Bat     *Archaeopteryx*     Pigeon

**FISHY LIZARD**
*Ichthyosaurus* (meaning "fish-lizard") was about 7 ft (2 m) long, with a streamlined body shaped like a dolphin. Paleontologists think it could reach a speed of 25 miles (40 km) per hour for short bursts.

### IN THE SEA

The pliosaur *Peloneustes*, 10 ft (3 m) long, had a short neck but a long jaw full of rounded teeth.

The turtle *Archelon* was almost 13 ft (4 m) long— as big as an automobile.

Triassic *Nothosaurus*, 10 ft (3 m) long, was at home in the water and on the land.

The lizard *Platecarpus* was 13 ft (4 m) long, with a tail as long as its body.

Cretaceous *Deinosuchus* was a giant crocodile, 49 ft (15 m) long.

## STRANGE BUT TRUE

Eric, a 5-ft (1.5-m) long Jurassic pliosaur from Queensland, Australia, is one of the most spectacular fossils in the world. As Eric's bones decayed, they were gradually replaced by minerals that formed a precious stone called opal.

*Discover more in* Surviving Relatives

**A VIEW OF THE WORLD**
In the Triassic Period, the continents fitted together into one huge continent called Pangaea. Fossils show that most dinosaurs lived near the center of Pangaea, the area now divided among North America, Africa and northern Europe.

Ginkgo tree

*Coelophysis*

## • THE ARRIVAL OF THE DINOSAURS •
# The Triassic World

The Triassic Period was the "Dawn of the Dinosaurs." The Earth was a huge supercontinent called Pangaea (from the Greek meaning "all Earth"), which had three main environments and was dominated by mammal-like reptiles. Near the coasts, forests of giant horsetail ferns, tree ferns and ginkgo trees were alive with insects, amphibians, small reptiles (such as the first turtles, lizards and crocodiles), and early mammals. The dry, cool areas near the equator had forests of tall conifers (pine and fir trees) and palmlike cycads. The center of Pangaea was covered by hot, sandy deserts. Many different plants and animals developed in these varied climates. There was plenty of food for many life forms, especially one group of animals that first appeared 228 million years ago—the dinosaurs. These extraordinary creatures began to rule the Triassic world.

**THE CHASE**
In the warm, moist forest close to the coast of Pangaea, two *Coelophysis* chase a *Planocephalosaurus* up a tree.

**AN EARLY DINOSAUR**
*Eoraptor*, the earliest known dinosaur (a fossilized head is shown supported by a human hand), lived 228 million years ago in what is now South America. This fast, lizard-hipped animal did not have a flexible jaw, so it could not trap struggling prey. It probably scavenged food from animals killed by larger reptiles.

## STRANGE BUT TRUE
*Coelophysis* was an agile predator that used its strong, clawed hands to grab small prey. One fossil was found with the remains of a baby *Coelophysis* in its stomach. Did this Triassic hunter eat a member of its own species?

## TRIASSIC DINOSAURS

*Zanclodon* was a 20-ft (6-m) long, meat-eating carnosaur.

*Herrerasaurus* was a 10-ft (3-m) long, meat-eating coelurosaur.

*Procompsognathus* was a 4-ft (1.2-m) long, meat-eating coelurosaur.

*Saltopus* was a 2-ft (60-cm) long, meat-eating carnosaur.

Horsetails

Cycads

*Piateosaurus* was an 26-ft (8-m) long, plant-eating prosauropod.

## DINOSAUR DIETS

Before flowering plants appeared in the Cretaceous Period, plant-eating dinosaurs grazed on ferns and tree leaves. Many plants had tough, waxy coatings or spines to protect themselves.

Meat-eating dinosaurs such as *Eoraptor* and *Coelophysis* hunted insects such as cockroaches and dragonflies, frogs, mammal-like reptiles and even early mammals—our distant ancestors.

Dragonfly

Tree fern    *Wielandiella*    *Haramiya*

*Discover more in* Meat-eating Dinosaurs

15

As the two supercontinents moved apart, the centers of dinosaur evolution spread. Most of the plant-eating sauropods, for example, remained in Gondwana, but some theropods, such as *Allosaurus*, spread throughout Laurasia.

Laurasia

Gondwana

FOSSIL SITES OF JURASSIC DINOSAURS

Tree ferns

## STRANGE BUT TRUE

The forests that covered the Jurassic world survive today—as seams of coal. Dead trees (even whole forests destroyed by storms or floods) were covered by mud and soil. They slowly hardened into material that looks like rock, but burns like wood!

**REARING ITS HEAD**
A *Diplodocus* rears to defend itself against a predator. Its clawed front feet and lashing tail are ready for battle.

• THE ARRIVAL OF THE DINOSAURS •

# The Jurassic World

Toward the end of the Triassic Period, the supercontinent of Pangaea started to divide into two smaller, but still very large, continents—Laurasia and Gondwana. New kinds of dinosaurs began to evolve on these new continents as they moved further apart. The slightly cooler temperatures and higher rainfall of the Jurassic world created a warm, wet climate that was ideal for reptiles. The lizard-hipped dinosaurs continued to break into the two groups that first split in the Triassic Period: the meat-eating theropods, which walked on two legs; and the plant-eating sauropods, which moved on all fours. The bird-hipped dinosaurs remained plant eaters. Giant, long-necked, plant-eating sauropods; plated, bird-hipped dinosaurs such as *Stegosaurus*; and bird-hipped plant eaters such as *Camptosaurus* were some of the mighty dinosaurs roaming the Jurassic world.

16

Camptosaurus, 20 ft (6 m) long, from Europe and North America

Allosaurus, 39 ft (12 m) long, from North America

Stegosaurus, 30 ft (9 m) long, from North America

Coelurus, 7 ft (2 m) long, from North America

## A SIZABLE APPETITE

Brachiosaurus was 39 ft (12 m) high and 75 ft (23 m) from nose to tail. It weighed an incredible 78 tons (80 tonnes)—as much as 12 African elephants—and ate the equivalent of 35 bales of hay a day. Its front legs were longer than its hind legs, and its whole body sloped downward from the shoulders (like a giraffe today), so its long neck could reach the tasty young leaves at the tops of the tallest trees.

Cycads

**FOOD FOR DINOSAURS**
Jurassic dinosaurs ate many animals, including freshwater turtles such as *Pleisochelys* and perhaps even the earliest bird, *Archaeopteryx*.

Ground cover ferns

*Discover more in* Long-necked Dinosaurs

17

**MOVING CONTINENTS**
Laurasia and Gondwana continued to move apart during the Cretaceous Period. By the end of this period, the outlines of the continents were roughly the same as they are today. There were land bridges between the continents, but dinosaurs tended to evolve separately on each of the land masses.

Conifer forest

Magnolias

• THE ARRIVAL OF THE DINOSAURS •

# The Cretaceous World

The Cretaceous Period lasted for 80 million years. More dinosaur species evolved in this time than in all the other dinosaur periods put together. But at the end of this period, about 65 million years ago, the dinosaurs disappeared. The early Cretaceous Period was warm. Winters were mild and dry, and most of the rain fell in summer. Later, summers became hotter and winters were colder in the temperate and polar regions. The giant plant eaters disappeared and were replaced by smaller species such as *Triceratops* and the duckbilled dinosaurs. Flowering plants evolved during this period (giant plant eaters during the Jurassic Period ate and trampled down so much of the vegetation that it gave new plants the chance to grow) and were eaten by hundreds of new species of plant-eating animals. There was a huge amount of food to support an enormous number of animals. The animals that ate the flowering plants were also eaten by predators, from snakes (which first appeared in this period) to great predatory dinosaurs such as *Tyrannosaurus*.

**PREDATORS AND PREY**
In this scene from the late Cretaceous Period in Mongolia, a *Velociraptor* (above right) battles with a *Protoceratops*, squashing dinosaur eggs in the process. An inquisitive *Prenocephale* looks on at the fierce encounter.

## THE CYCLE OF LIFE

Flowering plants (**A**) were pollinated by insects (**B**), which were eaten by small mammals such as *Alphadon* (**C**), which in turn were eaten by dinosaurs such as *Dromaeosaurus* (**D**). Dinosaur droppings fertilized plants, and the cycle continued.

D

A

B

C

## RELATED BUT NOT ALIKE

Animals that belong to the same family can evolve quite differently if they become isolated. *Hypacrosaurus* and *Bactrosaurus* were both duckbilled dinosaurs, and may have evolved from the same ancestor. But *Hypacrosaurus*, which lived in North America, was 30 ft (9 m) long and had a semi-circular crest on its head. *Bactrosaurus*, from central Asia, was only 13 ft (4 m) long. When the continents drifted apart, these dinosaurs evolved in different ways because they lived in such different places.

*Tyrannosaurus*

*Saltasaurus*

*Triceratops*

*Corythosaurus*

*Pachycephalosaurus*

*Euoplocephalus*

# Meat-eating Dinosaurs

**THE PREDATOR KING**
*Tyrannosaurus* ("the tyrant lizard") was the largest predator ever to walk the Earth. This gigantic creature weighed more than an African elephant. Five complete specimens of *Tyrannosaurus* have been found around the world.

Many carnivorous dinosaurs were powerful, fast hunters that ate prey larger than themselves. But there were also smaller meat eaters (*Compsognathus* was no taller than a chicken) that ate eggs, insects, small reptiles and mammals. Carnosaurs, ceratosaurs and coelurosaurs, the three main groups of meat-eating dinosaurs, all had short, muscular bodies, slender arms, and low, powerful tails that balanced strong back legs with birdlike feet. With large eyes and daggerlike teeth, they were formidable predators: the coelurosaur *Deinonychus* had long, slashing claws on its front legs that could rip open a victim's belly; *Megalosaurus,* a carnosaur, had powerful hinged jaws that were armed with curved, saw-edged fangs. Meat-eating dinosaurs had much larger brains than plant-eating dinosaurs. Hunting prey that was large and sometimes armored required good vision and an ability to plan an attack.

Eye

Nostril

Teeth

**A MEAT-EATER'S SKULL**
*Allosaurus*, a 39-ft (12-m) long predator from the late Jurassic/early Cretaceous Period, weighed more than a ton. Its skull could be up to 3 ft (1 m) long. As its jaws were hinged, *Allosaurus* could swallow large pieces of flesh whole.

**FIGHTING FOR LIFE**
*Tenontosaurus*, a plant eater from the early Cretaceous Period, fights a pack of ferocious *Deinonychus*. This reconstructed scene may well have happened. In the United States, the fossil skeleton of a *Tenontosaurus* was found surrounded by five scattered specimens of *Deinonychus*.

**TEETH AND JAWS**
Theropods, such as *Megalosaurus*, had long jaws that were usually armed with sharp, serrated teeth. New teeth were ready to replace those that wore out.

*Compsognathus*
Coelurosaur

*Oviraptor*
Coelurosaur

*Albertosaurus*
Carnosaur

## TOOLS OF EATING

The coelurosaur *Compsognathus* caught and ate prey with its hands. *Oviraptor* cracked open eggs with its beak. *Albertosaurus* had such short arms it had to tear off chunks of flesh with its powerful jaws. Scientists believe that the fish-eating *Baryonyx*, a theropod dinosaur discovered only in 1983, used the huge, hooklike claw on its hand to spear its prey.

*Baryonyx*
(not placed in a group)

## CUTTERS AND CHOPPERS

The shape of plant-eaters' teeth varied according to their diets. Dinosaurs that ate the hard leaves and fruit of cycads, palms and conifers had thick, peg-shaped teeth. Those that ate the leaves and fruit of softer, flowering plants had thinner, leaf-shaped teeth.

Peg-shaped tooth    Leaf-shaped tooth

Triassic dinosaurs ate horsetail ferns as big as trees.

Jurassic dinosaurs ate pine cones and cycad fruits.

Cretaceous dinosaurs ate flowering plants such as magnolias.

## STOMACH STONES

Sauropods, such as *Saltasaurus*, had no grinding teeth. They nipped off leaves with their slender, pencil-like teeth and ground them up with stomach stones called gastroliths. These were ground together by the muscular action of the stomach and crushed tough plant material.

## DINOSAUR DINNERS

New varieties of plants evolved on the Earth along with new species of dinosaurs. The plant-eating sauropods, the biggest dinosaurs of all, had to eat huge quantities of plants to provide them with enough energy.

## FINGER FOOD

*Othnielia*, a 5-ft (1.4-m) long gazelle-like dinosaur from the late Jurassic Period, used its five-fingered hands to push aside and hold down a fern while eating it. *Othnielia* had cheek pouches to store food so the tough plant material it ate could be chewed thoroughly later on.

• A PARADE OF DINOSAURS •

# Plant-eating Dinosaurs

For most of the dinosaur age, the climate was warm and moist, and plants grew in abundance. Hundreds, perhaps thousands, of species of plant-eating dinosaurs grazed on the ferns, cycads and conifers of the Triassic and Jurassic periods, then on the flowering plants of the Cretaceous Period. The bird-hipped ornithopods (the pachycephalosaurs, iguanodonts, duckbills, armored dinosaurs, and the horned dinosaurs that roamed in huge herds during the late Cretaceous Period) had special cheeks to store plants while they were busy chewing. The lizard-hipped sauropods, which included *Apatosaurus*, *Diplodocus* and *Brachiosaurus*, reached the lush vegetation at the tops of the trees with their long necks. These enormous plant eaters had large fermenting guts and stomach stones (as discussed above) that helped them digest huge amounts of plants.

## TEETH AND BEAKS

Paleontologists can tell much about how a dinosaur lived from the shape of its teeth or its beak, if it had no front teeth. Giraffes' teeth are different from zebras' teeth because giraffes eat tender leaves from the tops of trees, while zebras eat tough, dry grass. In the same way, different families of dinosaurs evolved different kinds of teeth and beaks to cope with a variety of plants.

*Protoceratops*, one of the smaller horned dinosaurs, had a parrotlike beak for shearing off plant stems, and scissorlike teeth to slice up its food.

*Camarasaurus*, an 59-ft (18-m) long sauropod, had spoon-shaped cutting teeth but no grinding teeth. However, it could reach high into trees to tear away leaves.

*Corythosaurus*, a duckbill, tore off leaves with its horny beak, stored them in its cheek pouches, then used rows of strong interlocking teeth to grind them.

*Plateosaurus*, an early, long-necked giant, had leaf-shaped teeth to pluck off the leaves of soft plants such as ferns. It did not have grinding teeth.

*Iguanodon* grazed on tough plants such as horsetails, and used its horny beak to nip off leaves. Its rows of ridged, grinding teeth crushed the leaves into a pulp.

## STRANGE BUT TRUE

*Heterodontosaurus*, a plant eater from the early Jurassic Period, had three kinds of teeth. In the front upper jaw it had small cutting teeth; on the lower jaw it had a horny beak. Then it had two pairs of large, fanglike teeth, with grinding teeth at the back.

# Long-necked Dinosaurs

The biggest, heaviest and longest land animals that have ever lived were the long-necked sauropod dinosaurs. These strange creatures had long tails, compact bodies, small heads, front legs that were shorter than the hind legs, and clawed first fingers or thumbs that were much larger than their other fingers (they may have used these to hook branches). In 1986, paleontologists unearthed a few bones from an enormous sauropod named *Seismosaurus* ("earthquake lizard") that may have been more than 98 ft (30 m) long. They have also discovered complete skeletons from sauropods almost as large. *Brachiosaurus,* for example, grew to 75 ft (23 m), stood 39 ft (12 m) high and weighed as much as 12 African elephants. *Brachiosaurus* and the other giants had pillarlike legs to support their great weight, but their skeletons were very light. Their bodies were shaped like giant barrels, and they carried their long tails high off the ground. *Diplodocus'* tail ended in a thin "whip;" other sauropods may have had tail clubs for self-defense.

**LONGEST NECK**
*Mamenchisaurus* had the longest neck of any known animal—an amazing 36 feet (11 m). It could hardly bend its neck, but it could rear up on its hind legs to reach the tops of the highest trees.

**MIGRATING HERDS**
Trackways (fossil footprints) and groups of fossils indicate that many sauropods lived in herds and may have migrated to find fresh food, with the adults protecting their young from predators.

**Small head**
A small head and a small mouth meant *Diplodocus* had to spend a lot of time eating to nourish its huge body.

**Strong but light**
Struts of bone and air spaces kept *Diplodocus'* skeleton light but strong.

**Long legs**
With the help of its long front legs, this grazer could reach the tender young leaves in the treetops.

**Strong legs**
*Diplodocus'* hind legs were almost solid pillars of bone to support the weight of its intestines and tail muscles.

**LONGER BUT LIGHTER**
*Diplodocus* was longer than *Brachiosaurus,* but weighed only a third as much—partly because the skeleton of *Diplodocus* contained air spaces that reduced its weight but not its strength. The head of a *Diplodocus* was no larger than that of a horse, but its neck was 23 ft (7 m) long and its tail stretched an incredible 46 feet (14 m).

**LONGER NECK**
*Brachiosaurus* carried its tiny head high off the ground on the end of a 20-ft (6-m) long neck. Its front legs were almost as long as its hind legs, which gave its already long neck extra reach.

## STRANGE BUT TRUE
Although sauropods did not need water to support their weight, apparently they could swim. One trackway seems to show *Diplodocus* walking only on its front feet. It must have been floating in water, pushing itself along with its front feet.

## FIT FOR A KING
In 1905, American millionaire Andrew Carnegie presented a plaster cast of *Diplodocus* to the Natural History Museum in London. He had financed the excavation of the original specimen. King Edward VII was there to unwrap the biggest present any king has ever received! Ten copies of the skeleton were sent to other museums around the world.

**Whiplash**
*Diplodocus* could injure or stun predators with the bony tip of its 46-ft (14-m) long tail.

**Muscular tail**
*Diplodocus* could not outrun a predator, but its great size and heavy, strong tail protected it.

**LONG NECK**
A modern giraffe, like all mammals, has only seven neck vertebrae. Sauropods, however, had between 12 and 19 neck vertebrae—all with bony struts to provide extra support.

# Armored, Plated and Horned Dinosaurs

Many plant-eating dinosaurs evolved in strange ways to defend themselves against predators or to fight over mates and territories. Pachycephalosaurs, for example, had domed-shaped heads with thick, strong layers of bone. The plated and armored stegosaurs were slow-moving, small-brained ornithischians that relied on spikes and armor plating to defend themselves. The best known are *Stegosaurus*, a 30-ft (9-m) long, late Jurassic dinosaur that had one or two rows of plates along its back, and two to six pairs of long, sharp spikes at the end of its strong tail; and *Ankylosaurus*, a 33-ft (10-m) long, late Cretaceous dinosaur that was protected by hundreds of bony nodules (some of them with spiky bumps) on its back and sides and a double-headed club of bone on its tail. The ceratopians, or horned dinosaurs, were the last group of ornithischians to evolve before the dinosaurs died out at the end of the Cretaceous Period. They lived for only 20 million years or so, but spread out across North America and Asia. Ceratopians formed vast herds and used their platelike, horned heads to protect themselves and their young against predators such as *Tyrannosaurus* and *Velociraptor*.

**PREDATORS BEWARE!**
*Styracosaurus,* a 16-ft (5-m) long ceratopian, defends its young from a predator by displaying its nose horn and spiked head shield. Its spiky frill protected its neck, and it could use its nose horn to rip open a predator's belly.

**BIG BUT LIGHT**
*Chasmosaurus'* head shield was light and easy to move. It was designed more for display than defense, since this animal could easily outrun predators.

**SMALL
BUT STRONG**
*Centrosaurus*, a 20-ft (6-m) long ceratopian, was a slow-moving animal that defended itself with its short, heavy head shield.

## BODY ARMOR
*Kentrosaurus*, a 16-ft (5-m) long stegosaur from Africa, had seven pairs of plates from the neck to the middle of the back, and seven pairs of spikes on its back, hips and tail.

## SPIKES AND SPINES
*Polacanthus*, a 13-ft (4-m) long nodosaur, protected its head and vital organs with a double row of vertical spines and used its strong, spiked tail for self-defense.

## DISHES AND DAGGERS
*Stegosaurus* may have used its back plates for defense, or for heating and cooling, but its tail spikes were used for self-defense. They were fused to the bones of the tail, so *Stegosaurus* could swing its spiky tail to scare off a predator.

## BUILT FOR DEFENSE

An ankylosaur *Euoplocephalus* from the late Cretaceous Period moved slowly and had a small brain. It could not hope to outwit fast, intelligent predators such as *Velociraptor*. But 20-ft (6-m) long *Euoplocephalus* was very heavily armored—even its eyelids were protected by bony shutters. It could cause serious damage with the club at the end of its 8-ft (2.5-m) long tail.

## A HOLLOW CREST

A male *Parasaurolophus* could stay in touch with other members of the herd or bellow a challenge to another male by forcing air from its mouth up into its hollow crest, then out through its nostrils. It must have had flaps or valves inside the crest to stop it from hooting whenever it breathed.

• A PARADE OF DINOSAURS •

# Duckbilled Dinosaurs

The duckbilled dinosaurs (hadrosaurs) had broad, ducklike beaks. They walked or ran on their hind legs, and leaned down on their shorter front legs to graze on vegetation. There were many species of duckbills; they were the most common and widespread plant-eating dinosaurs of the late Cretaceous Period. Hadrosaurs probably evolved in central Asia, but spread to Europe and North America. They had a varied diet, which meant they were able to survive as the Cretaceous climate became drier. All hadrosaurs were closely related, but they looked very different from each other. Some may have had inflatable nose sacs so they could communicate with each other by hooting. Others had hollow crests that acted like echo chambers. They could bellow or call each other by making noises that may have sounded like those made by a modern bassoon (above left).

# HEAD OF THE FAMILY

Paleontologists used to believe that duckbills with different crests belonged to different species. Now they think these different-crested duckbills were members of the same species. A female *Parasaurolophus*, for example, had a medium-sized, curved crest; a young, or juvenile *Parasaurolophus* had a short, fairly straight crest; and an adult male had a long, curved crest. All used their hollow crests to produce sounds that other members of the herd would understand.

Adult
male

Adult
female

Juvenile

## A DUCK'S BILL

Like all hadrosaurs, 43-ft (13-m) long *Edmontosaurus* had a toothless duckbill, covered with leathery skin, which it used to pluck leaves and fruits. It had rows of teeth in the back of its mouth, and it chewed food by moving its jaw up and down so the overlapping teeth crushed its food.

## CHOPPING AND GRINDING

Seen close up, *Edmontosaurus'* tooth rows consisted of scores of tiny, leaf-shaped teeth, which acted like a cheese grater.

## DID YOU KNOW?

*Saurolophus*, which had only a small, hornlike crest, may have produced noises by inflating a skin-covered sac on top of its nose. This would have been supported by the crest at the back of its head.

## LIVING TOGETHER

Like giraffes (which eat tree leaves) and zebras (which eat low-growing plants), flat-headed and crested duckbills were able to live together without taking one another's food supply.

*Discover more in* The Cretaceous World

# Record-breaking Dinosaurs

The dinosaurs were one of the world's most successful group of animals. They were the biggest, heaviest and longest land animals that have ever lived, and they dominated the Earth for almost 150 million years. Compared to this record, the four million years that humans have been on Earth seems like the blink of an eye. Dinosaurs were the world's strangest and most extraordinary animals. It has always been hard for people to imagine a world populated by such huge creatures: the remains of the first dinosaur ever described, 30-ft (9-m) long *Megalosaurus*, were first thought to belong to a human giant. It has also been hard for people to understand just how spectacular the dinosaurs were. *Seismosaurus*, the "earthquake lizard" and the biggest of the sauropods, may have been more than 98 ft (30 m) long. Only a few of its bones have ever been found: a 8-ft (2.4-m) long shoulder blade, taller than the biggest human giant; and a 5-ft (1.5-m) long vertebra. The ground must have quaked with each footstep from this gigantic creature.

## SMALLEST

*Compsognathus* was one of the smallest known dinosaurs. It was only 3 ft (1 m) long, weighed just 8 lb (3.5 kg), and stood no taller than a chicken. It must have been a swift and efficient hunter. One specimen was found with the bones of a tiny lizard in its stomach cavity.

## HEAVIEST

Weighing 78 tons (80 tonnes), 75-ft (23-m) long *Brachiosaurus* was as tall as a four-storey building. Its shoulders were more than 20 ft (6 m) off the ground and its humerus, or upper arm bone, was 7 ft (2 m) long. The humerus of an adult human is only about 1 ft (35 cm) long.

## DID YOU KNOW?

What do a *Struthiomimus* (whose name means "ostrich-mimic") and an ostrich have in common? They can both sprint swiftly on very long slim legs (an ostrich can outrun a horse) and have long thin necks with small heads.

## FASTEST

*Struthiomimus*, stood 7 ft (2 m) high and was 10–13 ft (3–4 m) long. It defended itself against predators by running at speeds of up to 31 miles (50 km) per hour, balancing on its long, birdlike hind legs.

## LONGEST NECK
*Mamenchisaurus*, at 72 ft (22 m), was almost as long as its close relative *Diplodocus*, but it had a fairly short tail. Its 36-ft (11-m) long neck, which it used to reach the tops of tall trees, is the longest neck of any known animal.

## LONGEST
With more than half of its total length of 89 ft (27 m) taken up by its 46-ft (14-m) long tail, *Diplodocus* was the longest known dinosaur. It would have used its strong, whiplike tail to defend itself against predators such as *Allosaurus*.

## BIGGEST PREDATOR
*Tyrannosaurus* was bigger than any predator except the sperm whale. It could grow up to 46 ft (14 m) long and was taller than a double-decker bus. It weighed 7 tons (7 tonnes).

## BIG, BIGGER, BIGGEST

In the 1970s and 1980s, fossil hunters found massive bones from sauropods even bigger than 75-ft (23-m) long *Brachiosaurus*. Called *Supersaurus, Ultrasaurus,* and *Seismosaurus,* these incredible animals may have been 98 ft (30 m) long! In this photograph, paleontologist Dr. James Jensen stands next to the reconstructed front leg of one of these giants. These fossils are still being unearthed, and it may take 10–20 years to reconstruct their skeletons. Then they will topple the record-breakers of today.

## MOST TEETH
*Anatotitan*, a duckbilled dinosaur, had about 1,000 tiny, leaf-shaped teeth arranged in rows of 200–250 on each side of its upper and lower jaws, all at the back of its mouth. Two mummified fossils of this species have been found, complete with the remains of their last meals: pine needles, twigs, seeds and fruits.

# Fossilized Clues

W e rely on fossils for clues about how dinosaurs lived. But dinosaur fossils are very rare. The chances of a plant or animal becoming fossilized were low because conditions had to be just right for fossilization to occur. An animal had to be fairly big (small dinosaurs had delicate bones that were easily scattered or destroyed, or eaten by scavengers), and it had to die in the right place. If a dinosaur's body was washed into a lake, for example, silt would cover it up quite quickly and its bones were more likely to be preserved. In most cases only the bones of the dinosaurs were preserved (a few turned into minerals such as opal), but occasionally the animal was covered by sand or volcanic ash that preserved, or mummified, the body and left an impression of the texture of its skin. Sometimes, only a dinosaur's footprints or its droppings have been preserved. Paleontologists use all these clues to piece together pictures of the creatures that lived so many millions of years ago.

**BACK IN TIME**
The deeper a layer of rock, the older it is. The oldest and deepest rocks contain single-celled bacteria and algae. More complex plants and animals are found in the newer rocks above.

**A FOSSIL IN THE MAKING**
A 20-ft (6-m) long *Camptosaurus* lies at the water's edge, dead of disease or old age. The hot sun has begun to dry the body, and if scavengers do not tear it apart, it will be covered by silt and gradually fossilized. The *Coelurus* shown here are eating the insects and other animals around the carcass. Their jaws are too weak for the thick skin of *Camptosaurus*.

Two American dinosaur detectives, Edward Cope (left) and Othniel Marsh (circled below), had a race to see who could unearth the most dinosaurs. They risked attack by Indians and paid "fossil rustlers" to steal specimens from each other. When they began their feud in 1868, only nine dinosaurs were known. By 1896, they had described 136 "new" dinosaurs between them.

**MYSTERY TEETH**
When Gideon Mantell saw the skeleton of an iguana's jaw, he realized that the mystery teeth, though much larger, were the same as the teeth of an iguana.

In 1834, a large number of *Iguanodon* bones were discovered in a slab of rock. Some of Mantell's friends paid £25 to buy the specimen for him.

**FIRST FINDS**
Englishman Gideon Mantell devoted most of his life to studying *Iguanodon*, the first dinosaur to be described in detail.

## DID YOU KNOW?

The first fossil remains of *Tyrannosaurus* were discovered in 1902, but none of the skeletons had the hands intact. Paleontologists had to wait until the late 1980s to discover that the greatest dinosaur predator of all actually had a two-fingered hand.

**FOUNDING FATHER**
Richard Owen described hundreds of ancient animals, from dinosaurs to the extinct moa—the biggest bird ever found—from New Zealand.

**NOT A GOOD LIKENESS**
Richard Owen drew this picture of *Megalosaurus* based on the few bones that had been found, as shown above.

• UNCOVERING DINOSAUR CLUES •

# Detective Work

In 1822, Mary Ann Mantell found some fossil teeth in a quarry. Her husband Gideon thought the teeth belonged to a giant plant-eating animal and began digging for more clues. Later, he found some foot bones. After more research, Gideon deduced that the teeth and bones belonged to an extinct reptile, which he called *Iguanodon* (meaning "iguana tooth"). He thought *Iguanodon* looked just like a giant iguana. Scientists, however, told him the teeth were from a rhinoceros and the bones were those of a hippopotamus. No-one had ever imagined that reptiles could have grown to be so big, or looked so different from modern lizards. When Richard Owen, an expert in animal anatomy, became interested in these curious fossils he realized that they came from a "new" group of animals, which he called dinosaurs. Owen's ideas led to "dinosaur-mania," and soon a new kind of scientist—the dinosaur detective—was kept busy unearthing "new" ancient reptiles.

**ON DISPLAY**
Expert reconstructions of dinosaur skeletons can tell us much about how these ancient animals looked. What we cannot see on display is the careful, patient work that goes into taking a fossil from the ground and recreating a skeleton in the museum.

• UNCOVERING DINOSAUR CLUES •

# Recreating a Dinosaur

Paleontologists dream of finding a complete dinosaur skeleton, but this rarely happens. Usually, they find a single bone—the basis of the painstaking process of recreating a dinosaur. In 1983, Englishman William Walker found a 1-ft (30-cm) long, curved fossil claw (left). Scientists believed the claw belonged to a large and previously unknown meat-eating dinosaur from the Cretaceous Period, which they called *Baryonyx* ("heavy claw"). They carefully removed all the fossilized bones they found, noting their exact location so they could put together a picture of how the animal looked when it died. After cleaning the bones, they "replaced" the missing pieces using their knowledge of other dinosaurs and living reptiles. Then they added layers of muscle and soon they had a vivid recreation of the dinosaur *Baryonyx,* which was almost as long as *Tyrannosaurus.* Reconstructed dinosaurs can be seen and studied in museums all over the world.

**Loose skin**
Today's meat-eating lizards and crocodiles have loose skin around the throat: the skin stretches so they can swallow large pieces of food. Like a crocodile, *Baryonyx* did not chew its food, so the skin of its throat probably looked like this.

**A fishy smile**
*Baryonyx's* lower jaw was curved like that of a fish-eating crocodile today, and contained 64 teeth—twice as many as other meat-eating dinosaurs. Scientists believe that it ate fish.

**IN THE SKIN**
Paleontologists recreated *Baryonyx's* skin by studying the skin of living reptiles such as snakes (above). Sometimes fossils show impressions of dinosaur skin.

## DID YOU KNOW?
Fossil bones and scales found in the area where *Baryonyx's* stomach would have been show that it ate fish such as 1-ft (30-cm) long *Lepidotes.* *Baryonyx* probably used the long, curved claws on its front feet to hook its prey from streams.

## Body building
Comparing the muscles of today's reptiles with dinosaur bones, paleontologists add layers of muscles beneath the skin to make a model of *Baryonyx's* body shape.

## A grasping grip
By looking at scars on bones, we can work out how even small muscles looked. This tells us that *Baryonyx's* arms were certainly strong enough to grasp a slippery fish.

## Quick digestion
As *Baryonyx* was a meat eater and digested its food quickly, its stomach was not as large as that of a plant-eating dinosaur. It had large stomach and chest muscles to help it run and twist its body when it was hunting.

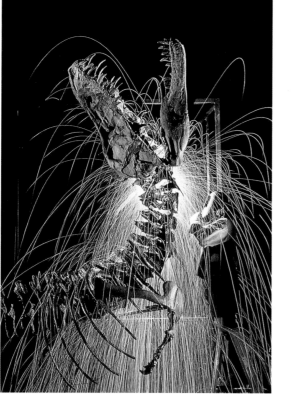

## FINISHING TOUCHES
Real fossils are so heavy and can be damaged so easily that the skeletons we see in museums are replicas, usually made of fiberglass and mounted on metal frames that are welded together. Sometimes the frames are hidden inside the replica skeleton.

## MISSING LINKS
Complete dinosaur skeletons are rare. Paleontologists often have to use small fragments and work out the shapes of missing bone by comparing the pieces they have with other fossils.

## MONGOLIAN FOSSIL SITES

Mongolia, in central Asia, is covered by sand and desert today. During the Jurassic and early Cretaceous periods, Mongolia was warm and moist, with lakes and shallow seas. Many species of dinosaur lived in this ideal environment.

## NORTH AMERICAN FOSSIL SITES

North America was warm and moist in the Jurassic and early Cretaceous periods. Great herds of plant eaters lived there, but they disappeared when the climate became colder and more changeable toward the end of the Cretaceous Period.

## BONES THAT ARE NOT BONES

Skeletons can fossilize in different ways. In a petrified fossil (right), preserved bones that form partial or complete skeletons have outer and middle layers that have been replaced by minerals. They literally "turn to stone." A cast is formed when mud fills the hollow spaces inside bones—this occasionally happens with a dinosaur's brain or the canals of its middle ear. The bone then rots away. Sometimes fossil skulls are hollow, and scientists can make a mold of the dinosaur's brain. Very rarely, a dinosaur is mummified in dry sand that gradually hardens into rock, leaving an impression of the animal's skin.

## OUT OF REACH

Beneath the surface of a lake, a dead dinosaur is safe from large scavengers. Its flesh rots away or is eaten by fish, and the skeleton remains intact.

## COVER-UP

Layers of sand or silt cover the dinosaur's bones, and stop them from being washed away.

## FOSSILIZATION

Trapped and flattened by layers of sediment, the dinosaur's bones are gradually replaced by minerals that are harder than the rocks around them.

## FOSSIL FINDS

Millions of years later, upheavals in the Earth's crust bring the dinosaur's fossilized skeleton close to the surface, where it is exposed by the weather and erosion.

*Discover more in* Skeletons and Skulls

# Skeletons and Skulls

**M**ost of the dinosaurs we know about were much bigger than even large modern mammals. An average-sized dinosaur such as *Camptosaurus* was about 21 ft (6.5 m) long—a third longer than an African elephant. But *Camptosaurus* weighed only about 3 tons (3 tonnes)—less than half the weight of an elephant. Dinosaurs had two distinct body types: a bipedal fast-running kind such as *Hypsilophodon,* and a quadrupedal heavy type such as *Camarasaurus.* They could grow to enormous sizes because their skeletons were superbly engineered; they were very strong without being very heavy. The vertebrae of the giant sauropods were supported by struts and thin sheets of bone because they were almost hollow; solid vertebrae would have made these animals too heavy to stand upright. Most dinosaurs had holes in their skulls. Meat eaters had the largest holes of all, to accommodate the bulging and powerful jaw muscles that opened and closed their jaws.

**Skull**
This 5-ft (1.5-m) long, lightly built "gazelle" of the dinosaur world had a horny beak at the front of its mouth, a fairly large brain and large openings for the eyes.

**Backbone**
Extra ribs in front of the shoulders supported the neck muscles.

*HYPSILOPHODON*

**Hands**
Four long, clawed fingers were used to grasp plant food or to support *Hypsilophodon* as it grazed on low-growing plants.

**Backbone**
Like the steel rods of a crane, the vertebrae provided support where it was needed most.

*CAMARASAURUS*

**Skull**
This 59-ft (18-m) long sauropod had a small head. The large openings on top of the skull may have helped to cool the small brain.

**Leg bones**
Like all sauropods, *Camarasaurus* had massive, pillarlike legs to carry its great weight.

**Chest**
Very deep ribs supported the large stomach *Camarasaurus* needed to digest its tough plant food.

**Hind feet**
*Camarasaurus's* toes could spread out for support as it reared up to reach young leaves in the treetops.

**Front feet**
Five strong, clawed toes helped to support the weight of the chest, neck and head.

**Restoring the bones**
Missing pieces of bone can be shaped by looking at bones from other animals. For example, the end of *Baryonyx's* ischium has not been found in fossil form, but paleontologists guessed what it looked like by examining the hips of other meat-eating dinosaurs.

**Muscle power**
Long "fins" of bone above and below the tail bones supported muscles that held *Baryonyx's* tail off the ground. These helped *Baryonyx* keep its balance as it ran or reached into the water to catch fish.

## STARTING FROM A BONE

Bones carry signs of the flesh that was once attached to them. Some have scars that show where the muscles connected to the bones. Paleontologists study these bones to build up a picture of how an animal looked and moved. This metatarsal, a long bone from the foot, belongs to an *Iguanodon*. Paleontologists used this bone to begin an accurate reconstruction of the skeleton of this dinosaur.

**Scientific illustration**
As the shading and shadowing on fossil bones is very fine, scientific illustrators use a stippling, or dotting, technique to make accurate drawings of fossils.

## FITTING BONES TOGETHER
Before they do this, scientists examine each fossil through a microscope, then clean them with air-powered tools or dental drills.

## ON THE DRAWING BOARD
Every fossil bone is drawn and described very carefully, so even scientists in other parts of the world know exactly what was found. The illustrations and descriptions of *Baryonyx* helped scientists decide that this unusual dinosaur belonged to its own dinosaur family.

## DRILLING FOR SCIENTIFIC GOLD

Fossils are rarely found in clay or soft sandstone. Most rocks are so hard that scientists have to drill out bone fragments, or even break up big pieces of rock with very carefully placed explosives.

## TYRANNOSAURUS UNFOLDS

Scientists spend months carefully preparing a fossil for reconstruction. They rely on their knowledge and experience to uncover the "real" dinosaur fossil from its wrapping of stone.

## CHIPPING AWAY

Most of the tools paleontologists use, such as hammers and chisels, trowels and paintbrushes, can be found in any hardware store.

**Based on the evidence**
Paleontologists found only a few fragments of bone from *Baryonyx*'s tail, but they knew that it was a large theropod, like *Allosaurus*, and would have had a long, strong tail to balance its heavy body.

## PIECES OF THE PUZZLE

At the field site, paleontologists draw a map that shows exactly where every fossil fragment is found.

## AT THE SCENE

The only known fossils of *Baryonyx* (the bones highlighted here) were found in a clay pit in southern England. Scientists are still trying to work out how this dinosaur is related to others.

## HANDLE WITH CARE

Even though they are as hard as rock, fossils are very delicate. Each one is wrapped in plaster of Paris, like a broken leg, to protect it on its journey to the museum.

*Discover more in* Skeletons and Skulls

## FIRST IMPRESSIONS
After studying the bones, Gideon Mantell drew this picture of *Iguanodon*.

## SECOND GUESSING
Twenty-eight years later, *Iguanodon* was shown as a heavily built animal with four legs and the horn of a rhinoceros.

## THUMBS UP
When more than 30 *Iguanodon* skeletons were found in Belgium in 1877, scientists realized the dinosaur's "horn" was, in fact, a thumb spike.

## THE TRUTH OF THE MATTER
Thanks to fossil tracks, we know that *Iguanodon* could have walked upright on two legs and was possibly the most widespread of the dinosaurs. Specimens from the early Cretaceous Period have been found in Africa, North America, Europe, Asia and even in the Arctic.

### CERATOSAURUS

This 20-ft (6-m) long predator had a strong lower jaw and a high, narrow skull. Both had large cavities to make space for the huge jaw muscles that drove razor-sharp fangs.

### OURANOSAURUS

Although its jaw muscles were weak, *Ouranosaurus* was an efficient plant feeder. As it closed its mouth, the bones of the upper jaw moved apart, breaking up food with bands of cheek teeth.

# DINOSAUR BRAINS

Dinosaurs had small brains, but this does not mean they were stupid. Brain size is not the most important factor. Brain complexity and brain size in relation to total body size are far more important. *Iguanodon's* body was as big as a bus; its brain was no bigger than a goose's egg. *Iguanodon* did not need much intelligence to find its food of leaves and fruit. *Deinonychus*, however, had to see, smell and chase fast-running animals. Its brain was the size of an apple, even though its body was smaller than a car. But the "thinking" part of a dinosaur's brain, the cerebrum, was much smaller than a mammal's cerebrum, which meant that a dinosaur could not have learned new things as easily as a monkey or a dog could today.

Rhesus monkey

Iguanodon

**Tail**
Spines on the undersides of the tail vertebrae supported muscles that helped *Hypsilophodon* carry its tail off the ground.

**Leg bones**
*Hypsilophodon* was a fast runner. As its femur was very short, the long tibia and foot could swing forward to give the dinosaur great speed.

**Feet**
Long, strong toes like those of an ostrich gave *Hypsilophodon* a sure footing as it sprinted away from danger.

**IN THE NOSE**
*Corythosaurus* (left) may have drawn air in through the nostrils at the front of its snout and into its hollow crest to produce sounds. *Brachiosaurus* had nostrils on the top of its head, possibly to help keep its body cool.

# DID YOU KNOW?

*Stegosaurus's* brain was the size of a walnut. A cavity in the vertebrae above its hips may have housed a gland that produced energy-rich glycogen. This gave *Stegosaurus* a burst of speed if it needed to escape from a predator.

**BUILT FOR STRENGTH**
The tibia and femur of *Tyrannosaurus* were the same length, and had powerful muscles attached to them. *Tyrannosaurus* could charge at its prey with a sudden burst of energy, but its legs were not designed for a long chase.

*Discover more in* Plant-eating Dinosaurs

## ARMOR PLATING
Dinosaur skin, like that of living reptiles, was made up of scales, sometimes with bony lumps (called osteoderms) that provided protection against predators' teeth.

# Footprints and Other Clues

Fossilized teeth and bones tell us much about how dinosaurs looked and lived. But paleontologists also use other clues to piece together pictures of the dinosaurs' day-to-day lives. Skin impressions show that dinosaurs were protected against predators and spiky plants by a tough covering of skin. Fossil footprints, called trackways, tell us how dinosaurs moved about, and that sauropods, hadrosaurs and horned dinosaurs traveled in herds. The remains of nests show that dinosaurs built nests close to each other for protection against predators and scavengers. The fossils of eggs and even baby dinosaurs indicate how small these animals were when they hatched and how quickly they grew. The bones of adult dinosaurs give clues to their diet, injuries and the cause of their death, while fossilized dung provides information about what dinosaurs ate.

## TRACKING FOSSIL FOOTPRINTS
Footprints show that many dinosaurs traveled in groups. These *Apatosaurus* prints were made by five adults moving in the same direction.

## DAILY DIET
Coprolites (fossilized dung) have been found containing hard seeds, pieces of pine cones, and even plant stems.

## STORIES IN STONE
Small plant eaters stick close to a herd of long-necked sauropods as it migrates across the late Jurassic landscape of North America. Sharp-clawed theropods shadow the herd, hoping to pick off a sick or injured animal.

# TRUE COLORS

We will never know what color the dinosaurs were. Fossilized skin does not preserve colors, so the colors and markings we give dinosaurs are those from our imaginations. Some paleontologists believe plant-eating dinosaurs had dull, dark colours so predators could not see them. Meat-eating dinosaurs may have been dull colored too, so they could hide and ambush plant eaters. Other scientists think plant-eating dinosaurs (especially males) changed color at different times of the year (as imagined in these illustrations of the duckbill *Lambeosaurus*) to mate or to defend their territories.

## FOOTPRINT CLUES

Scientists can estimate how quickly each dinosaur was moving by calculating the length of its pace, the length of its stride and the length of the animal's feet and legs.

Length of stride

Length of pace

Length of foot

Q: What color would you choose for *Tyrannosaurus*?

## ON GUARD

The *Maiasaura* nests discovered by Dr. Horner were spaced about 23 ft (7 m) apart, the same length as an average adult, so *Maiasaura* had enough space to avoid accidentally crushing one another's eggs. However, they were close enough to protect the nests from possible egg thieves such as *Oviraptor*.

**Amniotic sac**
A fluid-filled bag cushioned the embryo.

**Chorion**
This membrane provided oxygen.

**Eggshell**
Dinosaur young developed inside a sealed container.

**Yolk sac**
This provided nourishment.

## A DINOSAUR NURSERY

Up to 25 eggs were laid in each *Maiasaura* nest, which was a 7-ft (2-m) wide, 3-ft (1-m) deep bowl scooped out of mud. The hatchlings were about 1½ ft (50 cm) long.

• LIFE AS A DINOSAUR •

# Raising a Family

Paleontologists used to think that dinosaurs did not look after their eggs or their young because very few dinosaur nests had been discovered. In 1978, however, Dr. John Horner found a duckbill dinosaur nesting site in North America, with dozens of nests spaced just far enough apart so that adult dinosaurs could guard their own eggs without stepping on another dinosaur's nest. He also found fossil eggshells and the fossils of 15 baby duckbills. The babies had already grown much larger than when they were born, but they had not left the nest because they were still being cared for by their parents. Dr. Horner called these dinosaurs *Maiasaura*, or "good mother lizards."

Paleontologists know that at least two meat eaters, *Troodon* and *Oviraptor*, laid eggs. Fossil eggs from the giant sauropods have been found in Europe, South America and China, but we do not know how these enormous creatures managed to lay their eggs safely.

Chicken's egg

Possible
theropod egg

*Oviraptor's* egg

Emu's egg

## BIG BODIES, SMALL EGGS
Dinosaur eggs were very small in proportion to their bodies. Very large eggs would have very thick shells, and these could never be broken by the hatchlings.

## A TERRIBLE EGG THIEF?

Many paleontologists believe that *Oviraptor*, a theropod from the late Cretaceous Period, stole eggs from the nests of other dinosaurs. Its strong jaws could have easily broken eggshells and crushed the bones of the young dinosaurs it caught with its clawed hands. The first *Oviraptor* fossil, discovered in Mongolia in 1924 with a clutch of eggs, seemed to confirm this belief. Paleontologists thought the eggs belonged to a *Protoceratops*, but new evidence has shown that the eggs did in fact belong to *Oviraptor*. The debate continues.

## DID YOU KNOW?
Microscopic examination of *Maiasaura* embryos and hatchlings shows that they had very poorly developed joints in their legs. They had to be cared for by their parents. Hypsilophodons (the cousins of hadrosaurs such as *Maiasaura*), however, had strong legs and could fend for themselves as soon as they hatched.

*Discover more in* Duckbilled Dinosaurs

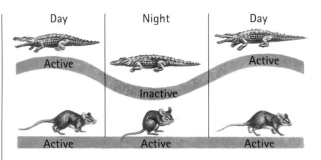

Active · Inactive · Active
Active · Active · Active

**UPS AND DOWNS**
A cold-blooded reptile, such as a crocodile, must bask in the sunlight before it is warm enough to move quickly. But a warm-blooded mammal, such as a mouse, can be active all the time. Its body temperature stays the same no matter how cold it is outside.

**Staying cool**
Spongy skin over the sail would have allowed heat to radiate quickly. Even a small drop in the temperature of the blooc would have helped *Ouranosaurus* to stay cool.

**Cooling the blood**
A complex system of small veins carried warm blood up into *Ouranosaurus'* sail, where it was cooled before it flowed back down into the body.

• LIFE AS A DINOSAUR •

# Keeping Warm; Keeping Cool

Every animal needs to keep its body temperature stable. If it cannot stay warm, it will not have enough energy to move around. If it becomes too warm, its brain may overheat and its breathing and digestion will not work properly. Dinosaurs had different ways to keep their bodies at stable temperatures. Some had frills, plates, sails or spikes to help them warm or cool their blood. Some scientists believe that dinosaurs may have had divided hearts to pump blood into their brains. This advanced body structure would probably have included an internal temperature control, or warm-bloodedness. The small, energetic meat eaters may have been warm-blooded, but this does not seem to be true for large, adult dinosaurs. Their bodies had a wide surface area, which meant they were able to radiate heat quickly and maintain a stable temperature.

**AIR CONDITIONING**
*Ouranosaurus* could warm up quickly in the morning, then cool down by the afternoon by pumping blood under the skin of the spiny "sail" on its back.

### HOT PLATES
*Tuojiangosaurus* had 15 pairs of bony plates along its back. Some paleontologists think the plates were covered by skin that was rich with blood to help the dinosaur warm up or cool down quickly.

### BIVALVES
A divided heart separates blood that flows under high pressure to the body from blood that flows under low pressure to and from the lungs. Some scientists think that tall or fast-moving two-legged dinosaurs needed a high-pressure blood supply to their brains and muscles.

Low pressure    High pressure

### NECKS AND TAILS
Sauropods had long necks to help them reach the treetops, and long tails to balance their long necks. Their necks and tails provided a large surface area to soak up heat from the sun or to cool them down in the middle of the day.

## A CHANGE IN TEMPERATURE
Scientists have looked at dinosaur bones under a microscope, and believe these reptiles may have been both warm-blooded and cold-blooded. Dinosaurs seem to have grown quickly (like warm-blooded mammals) when they were young, then more slowly (like cold-blooded reptiles) when they became adults. But small meat eaters, such as *Dromiceiomimus* (left), were very active predators, hunting lizards and insects. They would have needed a constantly stable temperature and may have been more warm-blooded as adults than other dinosaurs.

Nostril

## STRANGE BUT TRUE
Sauropods such as *Brachiosaurus* could "let off steam" when they became too hot by pumping blood through the delicate skin inside their huge nostrils. This cooled the blood so the rest of the body could then keep cool.

*Discover more in* What is a Dinosaur?

## A WIDE VARIETY
Like a duckbilled dinosaur, this rhinoceros has a wide mouth so it can eat many types of plants.

## SPECIAL DIETS
Like a horned dinosaur, this gazelle chooses its food carefully, plucking leaves and fruit with its narrow mouth.

**Into the mouth**
Paleontologists do not know if *Apatosaurus* had a muscular tongue or used its peglike teeth to rake leaves or twigs into its mouth.

**Down the neck**
Powerful muscles pushed food down *Apatosaurus'* 20-ft (6-m) long esophagus, a tube running from the mouth to the stomach.

**Living reptile**
Crocodile teeth are designed to grip, not cut.

**Large theropod**
*Tyrannosaurus* tooth

**Small theropod**
*Troodon* tooth

• LIFE AS A DINOSAUR •

# Eating and Digesting

Different dinosaurs ate and digested their food in various ways. Scientists have learned about these dietary habits by studying dinosaur teeth and bones, analyzing dinosaur dung and observing how living animals eat and digest their food. Paleontologists have found fossils of dinosaurs that sliced and ripped meat, dinosaurs that chewed plants or ground leaves into a paste before swallowing them, and toothless dinosaurs that ate eggs. The meat eaters had sharp teeth to cut up meat, which is easier to digest than coarse plants. *Tyrannosaurus'* sharp, serrated teeth were designed so that its prey's struggles actually helped it tear off chunks of flesh. Large plant-eating dinosaurs had internal features such as stomach stones (gastroliths) to help grind and digest the large quantity of plants they ate.

Upper jaw

Lower jaw

## CUTTING DOWN TO SIZE
*Styracosaurus* used rows of scissorlike teeth to snip leaves into small pieces.

## GRINDING TO A PASTE
*Edmontosaurus* used rows of grinding teeth to crush leaves into a paste.

## DID YOU KNOW?

A fossil of a large plant-eating sauropod has been found with 64 large, polished stones inside its ribs, which is where the stomach would have been when the dinosaur was alive.

## DINOSAUR DUNG

The dung of plant-eating dinosaurs was often hard enough to become fossilized. Paleontologists study fossil dung, or coprolites, to figure out what kinds of plants different dinosaurs ate. Coprolites can tell us how the sauropods grew to be so large before flowering plants evolved, and how large herds of duckbills could survive in the fairly dry conditions of the Cretaceous Period.

Esophagus

Spine

Rib

**Small intestine**
Microbes in the intestine might have helped to break down tough plant material so it could be absorbed more easily.

Kidney

Trachea

Lung

Heart

Liver

**Stomach stones**
Strong stomach muscles helped the gastroliths grind food into a pulp.

**Large intestine**
After food was broken down into a thick paste in the stomach, chemicals were absorbed through the walls of the large and small intestine (above).

**Cloaca**
*Apatosaurus* got rid of solid waste and urine out of a common opening called the cloaca.

*Discover more in* Footprints and Other Clues

49

## A SPIKY SHIELD

*Triceratops'* neck was a massive frill of solid bone with 3-ft (1-m) long horns that protected its neck and chest from an attack by another *Triceratops* or a predator.

## BUILT LIKE A TANK

*Euoplocephalus* was protected by bands of armor, bony studs on the shoulders and a heavy, bony skull. It could injure a predator by lashing out with a bony club at the end of its tail.

## STABBING TAIL

To defend itself against a predator, *Tuojiangosaurus* used its muscular tail, which was armed at the tip with two pairs of sharp spikes.

## DID YOU KNOW?

*Iguanodon* used its hand in many ways: for walking, for grasping food, for stripping leaves from branches and for self-defense. This peaceful plant eater could also use its thumb spike to injure or kill a predator by stabbing its neck or eyes.

## MULTI-PURPOSE TAIL

*Diplodocus'* tail was very long. It used the tail for support when it reared up to crush a predator with its front legs or swung it like a whip to blind or stun an attacker.

• LIFE AS A DINOSAUR •

# Attack and Defense

Many dinosaurs used their horns, spikes or armor to defend themselves. But even those without armor had their own defense weapons. *Apatosaurus* could rear up on its hind legs and crush an attacker with its front feet, or use its tail to injure a predator. Many sauropods travelled in herds, relying on safety in numbers so that only weak or sick animals would be attacked. The bird-mimic dinosaurs such as *Gallimimus* used their speed to escape, while *Pachycephalosaurus* could use its thick skull to defend itself against predators and other members of its own species. Meat eaters had speed, agility and sharp teeth for effective attack and defense. Large predators such as *Tyrannosaurus* hunted alone, and relied on a surprise rush. We will never know if dinosaurs used camouflage. Perhaps some species of plant eaters had dappled skin so they could hide from predators. Meat eaters may have used the same kind of disguise to ambush their prey.

## The Terrible Claw

Just as a falcon uses its razor-sharp claws to kill its prey, *Deinonychus* (whose name means "terrible claw") used the 5-in (13-cm), swivel claw on the second toe of each foot to kill its prey. It would leap into the air to kick or balance on one leg as it slashed at the skin of plant eaters. Fossils of five *Deinonychus* have been found beside the body of a *Tenontosaurus*, which suggests that the fast-moving, big-brained *Deinonychus* hunted in packs.

### BATTERING RAM

*Pachycephalosaurus'* skeleton was designed to withstand its charging attacks against other males, or predators.

### HEAD TO HEAD

Two 26-ft (8-m) long male *Pachycephalosaurus* are butting heads like mountain goats to see which will mate with a herd of females. Although protected by a solid dome of bone 10 in (25 cm) thick, one has become dizzy and is about to plummet to its death.

**BIG BANG**
According to one theory, several volcanic eruptions produced climatic changes that wiped out the dinosaurs.

**METEORITE HITS**
Perhaps a giant meteorite hit the Earth, causing dust clouds, acid rain, storms and huge waves.

**END OF AN ERA**
When the dinosaurs died out, all large land animals disappeared. Late Cretaceous mammals were small (*Alphadon*, shown here, was only 1 ft [30 cm] long) but evolved rapidly into thousands of new species to replace the dinosaurs.

# Why Did They Vanish?

The extinction of the dinosaurs 65 million years ago was the most mysterious and dramatic disappearance of a group of animals in the history of the Earth. But the dinosaurs were not the only animals to die out. More than half of the world's animals also disappeared, including the pterosaurs and large marine reptiles. The number of species of dinosaurs had been dropping for at least eight million years, but some species were common right up to the "K/T boundary," which marks the end of the Cretaceous Period and the beginning of the Tertiary Period. Some scientists believe that a volcanic disaster or a giant meteorite wiped out the dinosaurs. Others argue that such a disaster—causing disease, rising sea levels and gradual changes in climate—would have affected all animal life. Another theory combines these thoughts: changes in weather and sea levels had already reduced the amount of land and food for dinosaurs, and they were unable to cope with a sudden disaster.

## INTO THE FUTURE

Even today, habitat loss through earthquakes, storms or human activity such as clearing forests, is threatening the future of many animals.

## STRANGE BUT TRUE

People have produced some weird and wonderful theories to explain why the dinosaurs disappeared. Some suggest they died of boredom, "drowned" in their own droppings, were hunted by aliens, or even committed suicide!

## VICTIMS AND SURVIVORS

None of the current theories can explain why some animal groups disappeared, while others survived. Pterosaurs died out, but birds did not. Dinosaurs vanished, but small land reptiles and mammals survived. Mosasaurs, plesiosaurs and pliosaurs were wiped out, but turtles and crocodiles are still alive today.

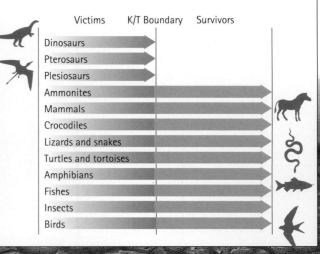

| | Victims | K/T Boundary | Survivors |
|---|---|---|---|
| Dinosaurs | | | |
| Pterosaurs | | | |
| Plesiosaurs | | | |
| Ammonites | | | |
| Mammals | | | |
| Crocodiles | | | |
| Lizards and snakes | | | |
| Turtles and tortoises | | | |
| Amphibians | | | |
| Fishes | | | |
| Insects | | | |
| Birds | | | |

# Surviving Relatives

**FEATHER FOSSILS**
The detailed impressions of feathers on this *Archaeopteryx* fossil confirm an important evolutionary link between reptiles and birds.

**SCALY SURVIVORS**
Crocodilians have hardly changed since the beginning of the Cretaceous Period. They have evolved slowly because they live in a stable environment.

Dinosaurs are dead, but it seems that certain dinosaur features live on in other animals. Dinosaurs and birds, for example, are very different animals but they have many characteristics in common. Scientists are now convinced that dinosaurs were the ancestors of birds. The skeleton of *Archaeopteryx*, the earliest known bird, was very similar to that of the lizard-hipped carnivorous dinosaur *Compsognathus*. Many scientists now classify *Archaeopteryx* as a small, flesh-eating dinosaur with feathers (fossilized feather shown left). Dinosaurs are also related to crocodilians, which survived the great extinction at the end of the Cretaceous Period. Crocodilians and dinosaurs have very similar skulls and common ancestors—the archosaurs. The dinosaurs disappeared, but crocodilians today are almost the same as their ancestors. Their way of life has changed little in 150 million years.

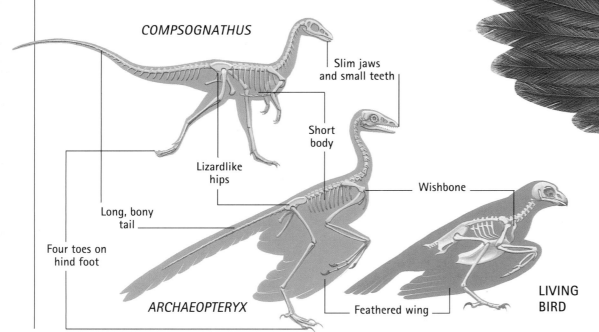

*COMPSOGNATHUS*

Slim jaws and small teeth

Short body

Lizardlike hips

Long, bony tail

Four toes on hind foot

Wishbone

*ARCHAEOPTERYX*

Feathered wing

LIVING BIRD

**FROM DINOSAUR TO BIRD**
Fossil records show a strong similarity between small carnivorous dinosaurs that ran upright on long, slim hind legs, *Archaeopteryx*, and living birds.

**FLIGHT PATH**

*Archaeopteryx* could fly by flapping its broad wings, but more often it would dive from its perch onto prey such as insects and small reptiles.

**FAMILY TREE**

*Ornithosuchus*

Alligators and crocodiles

Ornithischian dinosaurs

Saurischian dinosaurs

Birds

| TRIASSIC | JURASSIC | CRETACEOUS | TERTIARY | QUATERNARY |
| --- | --- | --- | --- | --- |

## RESEMBLING THE PAST

Hoatzin

Secretary bird

Some of today's birds are very similar to dinosaurs in their structure and behavior. The secretary bird of Africa rarely flies, but runs after insects, small reptiles and mammals on its hind legs—just as the dinosaur *Compsognathus* did. Baby hoatzins, from South America, use claws on the front of their wings to climb around in trees— just as *Archaeopteryx* did.

**INGENIOUS BUT INACCURATE**
In 1853, an *Iguanodon* was constructed in the Crystal Palace in London. It looked just like a giant, prehistoric iguana.

**REPTILIAN HUMANS**
If dinosaurs had not become extinct, would some have evolved to resemble humans?

# Myths and Tall Tales

Dinosaurs have been the subjects of myths and tall tales for years. When people first began to discover dinosaur fossils, they had many imaginative theories about the creatures that had such enormous bones. The earliest description of a dinosaur fossil came from China, almost 3,000 years ago. Chinese scholars thought the fossils were dragon bones. More than 300 years ago, a *Megalosaurus*' thigh bone dug up in England was believed to be the bone of an elephant, then a giant human. In 1820, a scientist thought that dinosaur trackways had been made by prehistoric giant birds. Dinosaurs died out 61 million years before humans appeared, but movies have shown them attacking people who lived in caves. In the past 50 years, however, we have begun to dispel many of the misunderstandings about these amazing animals.

## DRAGONS AND DINOSAURS

When Chinese scholars found dinosaur fossils, they imagined they belonged to great and powerful dragons, thought to bring good fortune to their people.

## DID YOU KNOW?

The ancient Chinese ground up dinosaur fossils to make powerful medicines and special magic powders. Even today, tiny amounts of these powdered "dragon bones" are used in some traditional Chinese medicines.

## CREEPING DINOSAURS

Early scientists could not believe that dinosaurs walked upright on straight legs. They thought these strange reptiles crept on sprawled legs.

## A STONE-AGE MYTH

Television has helped to keep myths alive by showing humans flying on pterosaurs, working with dinosaurs and even keeping them as pets.

## A DINOSAUR REVIVAL

People are understandably fascinated by dinosaurs. These diverse creatures ruled the world for 150 million years and were able to meet the challenges of a changing planet. Now, dinosaurs have "reappeared" in modern life. The box-office hit *Jurassic Park* stars a whole cast of plant- and meat-eating dinosaurs. A brightly painted reconstruction of *Allosaurus* (right) might be seen on the back of a car. You can also buy dinosaur balloons, cartoons, posters, stickers and books.

*Discover more in* Why Did They Vanish?

**Allosaurus**
Al-oh-sore-us:
"Different reptile"
Group: meat eater
Period: late Jurassic/early
   Cretaceous
Discovered: North America, 1877
Size: up to 39 ft (12 m)

**Plateosaurus**
Plat-ee-oh-sore-us:
"Flat reptile"
Group: plant eater
Period: late Triassic
Discovered: Europe, 1837
Size: 26 ft (8 m) long

**Coelophysis**
Seel-oh-fie-sis:
"Hollow shape"
Group: meat eater
Period: late Triassic
Discovered: North
   America, 1889
Size: 10 ft (3 m) long

**Coelurus**
Seel-ure-us:
"Hollow tail"
Group: meat eater
Period: late Jurassic
Discovered: North America,
   1879
Size: 7 ft (2 m) long

**Euoplocephalus**
You-op-loh-seff-a-lus:
"True plated head"
Group: plant eater
Period: late Cretaceous
Discovered: North America, 1910
Size: 20 ft (6 m) long

**Stegosaurus**
Steg-oh-sore-us:
"Roof lizard"
Group: plant eater
Period: late Jurassic
Discovered: United States,
   1877
Size: up to 30 ft (9 m)

**Saltasaurus**
Salt-a-sore-us:
"Salt reptile"
Group: plant eater
Period: late Cretaceous
Discovered: South
   America, 1970
Size: 39 ft (12 m) long

• THE END OF THE DINOSAURS •

# Identification Parade

Dinosaurs marched across 150 million years, and represented an amazingly successful and varied group of land animals. They prospered for many times longer than human beings have. Although we will never know exactly how many kinds of dinosaurs there were, we know enough about their evolution to see their steady progress from only a few species during the Triassic Period to almost twice as many during the Jurassic Period. This was followed by an incredible "flowering" during the Cretaceous Period, when there were more species of dinosaurs than during both preceding periods. Dinosaurs have taught us many valuable lessons about evolution and about how a group of animals spread across the land, and dominated the world before disappearing. But we are left with only tantalizing clues about how dinosaurs lived.

**Pachycephalosaurus**
Pack-ee-seff-ah-low-sore-us:
"Thick-headed reptile"
Group: plant eater
Period: late Cretaceous
Discovered: North America, 1943
Size: up to 26 ft (8 m) long

**Maiasaura**
My-ah-sore-ah:
"Good mother lizard"
Group: plant eater
Period: late Cretaceous
Discovered: North America, 1979
Size: up to 30 ft (9 m)

*Brachiosaurus*
Brak-ee-oh-sore-us:
"Arm reptile"
Group: plant eater
Period: late Jurassic
Discovered: North America, 1903
Size: up to 75 ft (23 m)

*Deinonychus*
Die-non-i-kus:
"Terrible claw"
Group: meat eater
Period: early Cretaceous
Discovered: North
America, 1969
Size: 10 ft (3 m) long

*Hypsilophodon*
Hip-sih-loh-foe-don:
"High-ridged tooth"
Group: plant eater
Period: early Cretaceous
Discovered: Europe, 1870
Size: 7 ft (2 m) long

*Ouranosaurus*
Oo-ran-oh-sore-us:
"Brave reptile"
Group: plant eater
Period: early Cretaceous
Discovered: Africa, 1976
Size: 23 ft (7 m) long

# DINOSAURS TODAY

When Richard Owen invented the name dinosaur 150 years ago, we knew of just nine species. Today we know of at least 1,000, which includes an incredible variety of plant eaters, meat eaters and egg thieves, dinosaurs with horns and crests, spikes and razor-sharp claws. We are surrounded by dinosaurs: in museums, movies and theme parks, such as this display of robot dinosaurs in Japan. Even though they disappeared 65 million years ago, dinosaurs are "alive" in our imaginations. We are still learning about them; in fact, children today know more about dinosaurs than most adults do.

*Tyrannosaurus*
Tie-ran-oh-sore-us:
"Tyrant lizard"
Group: meat eater
Period: late Cretaceous
Discovered: North America, 1902
Size: up to 46 ft (14 m)

*Parasaurolophus*
Par-ah-sore-ol-oh-fus:
"Parallel-sided reptile"
Group: plant eater
Period: late Cretaceous
Discovered: North America, 1923
Size: 33 ft (10 m) long

*Triceratops*
Try-ser-ah-tops:
"Three-horned face"
Group: plant eater
Period: late Cretaceous
Discovered: North America, 1889
Size: up to 30 ft (9 m)

*Struthiomimus*
Strooth-ee-oh-mime-us:
"Ostrich-mimic"
Group: meat eater
Period: late Cretaceous
Discovered: North America, 1917
Size: up to 13 ft (4 m)

# — Dinosaur Facts —

**Q** Could dinosaurs swim?

**A** Although dinosaurs were not related to the giant marine reptiles, we know that at least some species could swim, and many of the plant eaters probably grazed in swamps. Scientists were puzzled by a set of *Diplodocus* footprints that showed only the animal's front feet. Then they realised the sauropod was floating in water, pushing itself along with its front feet and steering with its back legs and tail (as above).

**Q** How do you become a paleontologist and dig up dinosaur fossils?

**A** To be a paleontologist, you need to study science, especially biology and geology, in high school and in college. You usually need a specialized research degree as well.

**Q** Where did dinosaurs live?

**A** Dinosaur fossils, and sometimes footprints, have been found on every continent, including Antarctica, which was not as cold during the Age of the Dinosaurs as it is today. Most parts of the world looked very different when the dinosaurs were alive. Slow geological changes have pushed up flat ground into steep mountains, and regions have become colder because continents have moved.

**Q** Did dinosaurs fly?

**A** No, dinosaurs could not fly, but there were some Mesozoic reptiles, such as *Pteranodon*, which could fly.

**Q** Did any dinosaurs eat both meat and plants?

**A** Paleontologists believe that some of the lizard-hipped dinosaurs, such as *Ornithomimus, Gallimimus* and *Struthiomimus*, probably ate small reptiles, mammals, insects—even other dinosaurs' eggs—as well as plants. Meat gave these gazelle-like animals the energy they needed to outrun predators. Speed was their only defense.

**Q** How can you tell a dinosaur's sex?

**A** It is very difficult to tell whether a dinosaur was male or female just from the bones. By looking at mammals, however, we can guess that male dinosaurs were generally larger than females, and it is likely that male duckbills (such as *Parasaurolophus* shown here) had larger crests. Fossils of *Pachycephalosaurus* show big differences in the size of the skull, and it seems that while both sexes had domed skulls, males had heavier heads for fighting, just like today's mountain goats.

Male

Female

**Q** Were dinosaurs affected by insects and parasites?

**A** Dinosaurs had thick, tough skins, but we are sure there were insects and ticks that bit them and sucked their blood—after all, today's crocodiles and monitor lizards are bitten by mosquitoes and blood-sucking flies. Although paleontologists have never found fossils of parasites inside dinosaur bodies, it is likely that parasites attacked dinosaurs just as they do animals today.

**Q** Were meat-eating dinosaurs smarter than plant eaters?

**A** Yes, meat-eating dinosaurs had larger brains than plant eaters, and needed intelligence to hunt or ambush large and sometimes heavily armoured prey.

**Q** How long could dinosaurs live?

**A** Paleontologists are unable to determine from fossil remains how long a dinosaur could live, but they do have some clues about how long it took dinosaurs to reach sexual maturity. Recent studies suggest that various dinosaurs, such as hadrosaurs, could breed somewhere between 5 and 12 years.

**Q** Why are fossil finds so exciting?

**A** They are incredibly rare. Some dinosaurs were the largest land animals ever to have lived on Earth, but large animals—whether they are reptiles or mammals—are not as common as small animals and their bones are therefore less likely to be found. Recently, the remains of many small dinosaurs were found in the Gobi Desert. But this was a very unusual find. Small animals can be torn apart by scavengers or eaten by insects. Their bones can be scattered by rain, or crushed by earth movements before they can become fossils. Even if these small bones are fossilized, they will be very hard to find and recognize millions of years later.

**Q** How many species of dinosaur were there?

**A** This is one question we will never be able to answer; only a few animals from any group are ever fossilized, so fossils give just a small "window" into the world of dinosaurs. About 800 species of dinosaur have been described but many of these may have been males and females from the same species and of different ages, so we probably know about only 350 genuine species of dinosaur. However, some scientists think there may have been between 1,000 and 1,300 species of dinosaur, while others estimate as many as 6,000 species.

**Q** Could dinosaurs sweat?

**A** No, their skin was scaly and did not have sweat glands, so they had other ways of keeping cool.

**Q** What do the names of dinosaurs mean ?

**A** The names of dinosaurs, like those of all animals and plants, tell us something about how each dinosaur is related to other dinosaurs. Names are made up from Latin and Greek words, and usually describe something outstanding about the animal. *Tyrannosaurus rex*, for example, means "king of the tyrant lizards;" *Corythosaurus* is "helmet lizard;" and *Protoceratops* stands for "first horned face."

**Q** Did prehistoric humans and dinosaurs live at the same time?

**A** Some movies may place humans and dinosaurs in the same prehistoric world, but humans evolved only 4 million years ago. This was 61 million years after the dinosaurs became extinct.

# Glossary

**ankylosaurs** Members of a group of late Cretaceous dinosaurs that spread throughout North America and East Asia. They were heavily armored with thick plates of bone, spikes and bony nodules in the skin of their back and sides. They had thick skulls and bony plates on top of the skull, and a club of solid bone at the end of the tail.

**archosaurs** A major group of reptiles that includes the living crocodilians as well as the extinct dinosaurs, pterosaurs and thecodontians.

**bipedal** Walking on two legs.

**carnosaurs** Large carnivorous, or meat-eating, theropod (saurischian) dinosaurs such as *Megalosaurus*, *Allosaurus* and *Tyrannosaurus*. Some paleontologists believe carnosaurs, which ranged from 16 ft (5 m) to 39 ft (12 m) long, were scavengers as well as predators. They were so large they did not have enough energy to chase plant-eating dinosaurs for very long.

**Cenozoic Era** This period began with the extinction of the dinosaurs 65 million years ago and is known as the Age of Mammals.

**ceratopians** Late Cretaceous horned dinosaurs that existed for 20 million years. Although ceratopians were the last group of ornithischian dinosaurs to evolve before the extinction of these ruling reptiles at the end of the Cretaceous Period, they established themselves all over western North America and central Asia, where they lived in large herds.

**ceratosaurs** Medium-sized theropods distinguished by the small crests or bony horns on their noses. Trackways made by *Ceratosaurus*, a late Jurassic predator from North America, indicated that these predators hunted in packs to bring down larger dinosaurs.

**coelurosaurs** Small, light carnivorous saurischians such as *Coelurus*, *Compsognathus*, *Gallimimus* and *Struthiomimus*. Coelurosaurs (the name means "hollow-tailed lizard") lived from the Late Triassic to the late Cretaceous Period in North America, Europe and Africa. These delicately built hunters ranged from 4-ft (1.2-m) long *Procompsognathus*, to 13-ft (4-m) long *Gallimimus*.

**coprolite** A dinosaur dropping that has fossilized.

**Cretaceous Period** The geological period from 145 to 65 million years ago. This period saw both the flowering and the extinction of the dinosaurs.

**crocodilians** The only living representatives from the archosaur group of reptiles. They include crocodiles, gharials, tomistoma, alligators and caimans.

**cycad** A primitive, palmlike tree that flourished in the Triassic and Jurassic periods. Only a few species survive today, and all of them are highly poisonous to mammals.

**evolution** Gradual change. New species of dinosaurs evolved over millions of years.

**extinction** The dying out of a species. Remaining dinosaurs species became extinct in the Cretaceous Period.

**Gondwana** The southern supercontinent formed when Pangaea split into two, which began about 208 million years ago.

**hadrosaurs** Duckbilled dinosaurs such as *Hadrosaurus*, *Maiasaura* or *Anatotitan*. Hadrosaurs were the most common and varied plant-eating ornithopods, and the greatest success story in the history of the dinosaurs. They evolved in central Asia during the early Cretaceous Period, and spread to Europe, North and South America.

**horsetail fern** Primitive, swamp-living plants related to ferns. Horsetails once grew as large as modern tree ferns, but only a few small species survive today.

**ichthyosaurs** Short-necked, dolphin-shaped marine reptiles that lived at the same time as dinosaurs. Ichthyosaurs gave birth to live young at sea–they did not come ashore to lay eggs. Ichthyosaurs evolved in the Triassic Period, and ranged from 3-ft (1-m) long *Mixosaurus* to 49-ft (15-m) long *Shonisaurus*. *Ichthyosaurus* grew to 7 ft (2 m) long and is known from many fossils, including coprolites and stomach contents.

**iguanodonts** Large, plant-eating, ornithopod dinosaurs. Iguanodonts evolved in the mid-Jurassic Period and spread throughout the world; their fossils have been found from the Arctic Circle to Australia. The group dominated the early Cretaceous Period, and 30-ft (9-m) long *Iguanodon* is its best known member.

*Tyrannosaurus*

Volcano

*Tuojiangosaurus*

Magnolia

Horsetails

*Euoplocephalus'* tail

**ilium** The main bone of the pelvis. The ilium supports the legs and is attached to the backbone.

**ischium** One of the bones of the pelvis. In dinosaurs, the ischium pointed downward and supported the muscles of the legs and tail.

**Jurassic Period** The second geological period in the Age of Reptiles. It lasted from 208 to 145 million years ago.

**Laurasia** The northern supercontinent formed when Pangaea split into two.

**mammals** A group of backboned animals that have hair and feed their young milk.

**Mesozoic Era** The Age of Reptiles that spanned the Triassic, Jurassic and Cretaceous periods. The Mesozoic Era lasted from 245 to 65 million years ago.

**metatarsal** One of the long bones (behind the toes) in the foot.

**meteorite** A rocklike object from the remains of a meteoroid that has fallen on Earth.

**mummified** Dried out by heat or wind.

**ornithischians** "Bird-hipped" dinosaurs. In this group the pubis pointed back and down, parallel to the ischium. All the ornithischian dinosaurs were plant eaters.

**ornithopods** "Bird-footed" ornithischian dinosaurs. This group included the pachycephalosaurs, iguanodonts, hadrosaurs and the horned, armored and plated dinosaurs.

**pachycephalosaurs** Plant-eating, late Cretaceous, ornithopod dinosaurs with skulls thickened into domes of bone. Pachycephalosaurs lived in Asia and North America and ranged from 7 ft (2 m) to 15 ft (4.6 m) in length.

**paleontologist** A scientist who studies ancient life, especially the fossils of plants and animals.

**Pangaea** The supercontinent that formed in the Permian Period and broke up during the Jurassic Period.

**petrified** Fossilized bone that has layers of bone replaced by minerals.

**plesiosaurs** Large marine reptiles of the Mesozoic Era. Plesiosaurs, which ranged from 8-ft (2.3-m) long *Plesiosaurus* to 46-ft (14-m) long *Elasmosaurus,* were generally long-necked.

**pliosaurs** Plesiosaurs with short necks and thick, powerful bodies.

**predator** An animal that hunts other animals (prey) for food.

**prosauropods** Late Triassic to early Jurassic ancestors of the long-necked sauropods. Prosauropods reached lengths of 7 ft (2.1 m) to 33 ft (10 m).

**pterosaurs** Flying reptiles, only distantly related to dinosaurs. Pterosaurs evolved during the late Triassic Period and had wingspans ranging from 1½ ft (45 cm) to 39 ft (12 m).

**pubis** One of the lower bones of the pelvis. In saurischian dinosaurs it pointed forward; in ornithischians it lay parallel to the ischium and pointed backwards.

**quadrupedal** Walking on four legs.

**saurischians** "Lizard-hipped" dinosaurs. In this group, the pubis pointed towards the head of the pelvis. The saurischian dinosaurs are divided into two-legged, meat-eating theropods and four-legged, plant-eating sauropods.

**sauropods** Large, plant-eating, saurischian dinosaurs. Sauropods evolved during the late Triassic Period, and included the largest land animals ever to have lived.

**species** A group of animals or plants that can breed with each other and produce young that can also breed. A group of similar species forms a genus.

**stegosaurs** Late Jurassic dinosaurs that had alternating or staggered rows of plates along their backs, and two pairs of long, sharp spikes at the end of their strong tails.

**theropods** Meat-eating saurischian dinosaurs that walked on their hind legs.

**trackways** A series of footprints that are left as an animal walks over soft ground.

**Triassic Period** The first period of the Age of Reptiles. The Triassic Period lasted from 245 to 208 million years ago.

**vertebrae** Bones from the back of the skull to the tail that protect the spinal column.

*Tuojiangosaurus'* tail

*Parasaurolophus*

Teeth of plant-eating dinosaurs

*Triceratops*

*Pleisochelys*

# Index

## Picture Credits

(t=top, b=bottom, l=left, r=right, c=center, F=front, C=cover, B=back, Bg=background)
Ad-Libitum, 28cl, 38tr, 45t (S. Bowey). **American Museum of Natural History,** 34tl (Neg. No. 28006), 41cr (Neg. No. 35423/A.E. Anderson). **Image Select,** 56cl (Ann Ronan Picture Library). **Ardea,** 11tc (M.D. England), 42tcl, 60bl (F. Gohier). **Auscape,** 55br (Ferrero/Labat). **Austral International,** 42tc (Keystone). **Australian Museum,** 48c (C. Bento). **Australian Picture Library,** 35br, 57br (P. Menzel), 52cl (NASA/Reuters). **Berlin Museum für Naturkunde,** 54tc (P. Wellnhofer). **Coo-ee Picture Library,** 6cl (R. Ryan). **Everett Collection,** 57bl. **Michael & Patricia Fogden,** 35cr. **The Image Bank,** 53tr (J. Hunter), 52tl, 62cl (Image Makers). **Institut Royal des Sciences Naturelles de Belgique,** 39tr. **Matrix,** 54tl (Humboldt Museum, Berlin/ L. Psihoyos), 20bl (The Natural History Museum, London/L. Psihoyos), 31cr (L. Psihoyos), 20bl (The Natural History Museum, London/L. Psihoyos), 31cr 36bl, 38tc, 49tr, 57bcr, 59tr (L. Psihoyos). **The Natural History Museum,** London, 11tr, 13tr, 22c, 22tl, 24/25b, 25c, 34bl, 34cl, 34ct, 34tr, 35cl, 36bcr,
37bl, 37tr, 38cl, 38br, 39tc, 39tl, 42cl, 42tl, 44bl, 48bl, 63cr. **Natural History Photographic Agency,** 48tcl (P. Johnson). **David Norman,** 56bl. **Peabody Museum of Natural History,** Yale University, 34cl. **The Photo Library,** Sydney, 33tc (SPL/S. Stammers). **Photo Researchers,** 38tl (T. McHugh). **Planet Earth Pictures,** 54cl (P. Chapman); 48tl (W. Dennis). **Stock Photos,** 55bcr (Animals Animals). **Tom Stack & Associates,** 11tl (J. Cancalosi), 35tl (S. Elmore). **University of Chicago Hospitals,** 14bl. **Wave Productions,** 37br (O. Strewe)

## Illustration Credits

Wendy de Paauw, 56/57t. Simone End, 4/5c, 5br, 9brc, 10tl, 17r, 19c, 19t, 22tl, 25tr, 27cr, 29cr, 29tl, 41bc, 43ct, 46tl, 47c, 47ct, 47tl, 47tr, 57cr, 58/59c, 60, 61c, 62cl, 62bcl, 63tcr, 63br, icons. Christer Eriksson, 20/21c, 26/27c, 31c, 50/51c, 52/53c, 54/55c. John Francis/Bernard Thornton Artists, UK,
14/15c, 16/17c, 18/19c. David Kirshner, 2/3b, 10bc, 10bl, 11bl, 11br, 11tc, 22/23c, 28/29c, 35–38c, 41tr, 48/49c, 48b, 55bl, 53br. Frank Knight, 5cr, 6bc, 13cr, 20cl, 23tr, 24bc, 27br, 29tr, 31br, 32tl, 33r, 38bl, 40, 40/41tc, 41tc, 47br. 50, 51ct, 51tl, 54bl, 62bl, 63bcr, 63tr. James McKinnon, 1, 8/9c, 8tl, 20tl, 24/25t, 24tr, 25br, 25c, 29b, 32/33b, 42/43b, 62tl. Colin Newman/Bernard Thornton Artists, UK, 4tl, 6/7c, 7t, 12/13b, 12tl, 13tl, 44/45cl, 44ct, 44tl, 45cr. Paul Newman, 53cr. Marilyn Pride, 15bc. Andrew Robinson/Garden Studio, 34/39c. Peter Schouten, 2tl, 4b, 5t, 15r, 17t, 19b, 21tr, 22bl, 23br, 26bl, 27tr, 30, 31t, 46/47c. Ray Sim, 14tl, 16tl, 18tl, 33t, 38bc. Rod Westblade, endpapers.

## Cover Credits

Christer Eriksson, FCc. Peter Schouten, FCtr, BCtl. Colin Newman/Bernard Thornton Artists, UK, FCtl. Frank Knight, BCbr. Quarto Publishing, Bg.